EMDR Coloring & Activity Book for Kids

EMDR stands for eye movement desensitization & reprocessing

An Interactive Resource to Help Kids Process Big Feelings, Get Unstuck from Tricky Memories, and Make Room for the Good Stuff in Life

Christine Mark-Griffin, LCSW
EMDR Consultant & Advanced Trainer

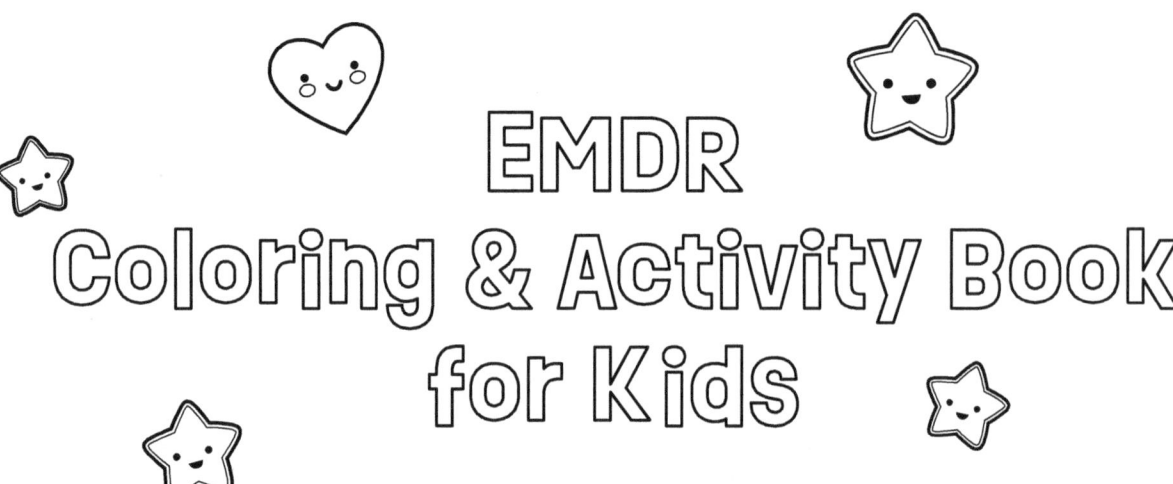

This book belongs to: _____

EMDR COLORING & ACTIVITY BOOK FOR KIDS
Copyright © 2025 Christine Mark-Griffin

Published by
PESI Publishing, Inc.
3839 White Ave
Eau Claire, WI 54703

Cover and interior design by Emily Dyer
Editing by Jenessa Jackson, PhD

ISBN: 9781683737902 (print)
ISBN: 9781683737919 (KPF)
ISBN: 9781683737926 (ePDF)

All rights reserved.
Printed in the United States of America.

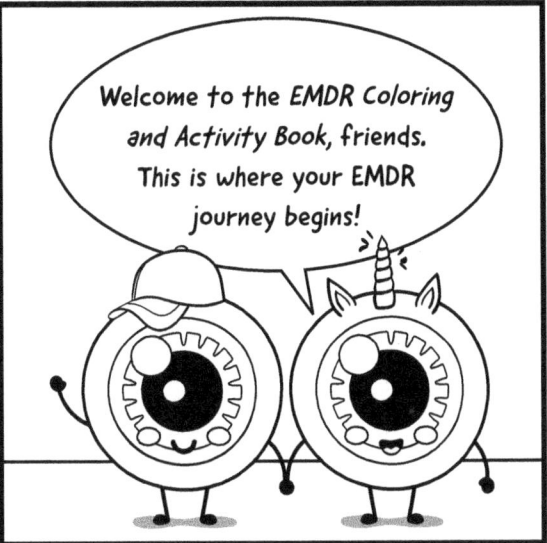

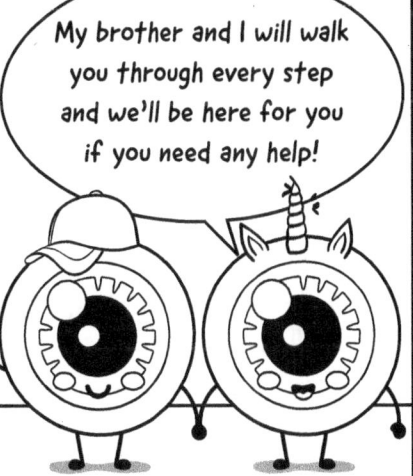

All of us have memories that make us want to cheer! Can you write or draw about your happy memories here?

A memory that makes you feel warm and fuzzy!

A memory where you felt unique!

A memory where you shined like a star!

A memory that feels sweet!

Let's figure out how big your problems are on a scale. Do they feel small like a fish or big like a whale?

A memory that makes you worry.

A memory that is upsetting.

A memory that makes you feel mad.

A memory that feels twisted!

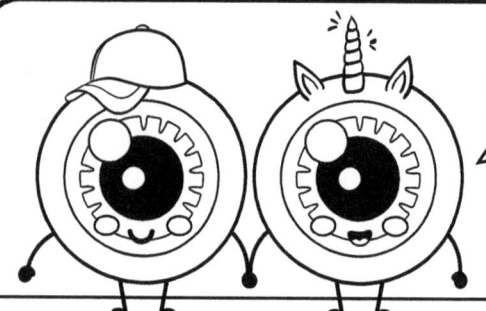

Lots of kids have problems that give them some trouble. Can you pick the ones that make you struggle?

- ☐ Nightmares
- ☐ Flashbacks
- ☐ Trouble sleeping
- ☐ Becoming startled
- ☐ Feeling angry
- ☐ Feeling annoyed
- ☐ Feeling worried
- ☐ Feeling sad
- ☐ Feeling scared
- ☐ Feeling numb
- ☐ Becoming aggressive
- ☐ Feeling on edge
- ☐ Bad thoughts about yourself
- ☐ Avoiding people or places
- ☐ Feeling like things are not fun anymore
- ☐ Having a hard time feeling happy
- ☐ Difficulty concentrating
- ☐ Blaming yourself or others
- ☐ Isolating
- ☐ Trouble eating

Below are some common thoughts that are pretty unhelpful. Check the ones that feel really stressful!

Unhelpful Thoughts

- ☐ I am bad.
- ☐ I am ugly.
- ☐ I am mean.
- ☐ I'm not smart.
- ☐ I'm not enough.
- ☐ I am worthless.
- ☐ I don't belong.
- ☐ I can't handle it.
- ☐ I am different.
- ☐ I'm not safe.
- ☐ I am angry.
- ☐ I can't ask for help.
- ☐ I am dumb.
- ☐ I can't learn.
- ☐ I always mess up.
- ☐ It is my fault.
- ☐ I can't do it.
- ☐ I am the worst.
- ☐ I don't matter.
- ☐ I need to be perfect.

Practice tracing back and forth here to make all your worries disappear!

Start here and trace to the right!

Trace to the left

Trace to the right

Trace to the left

Trace to the right

Let's imagine that you have a magical box where you can store all of your unhelpful thoughts! Or imagine a container in your mind to keep your problems in. You get to decide when to take them out and work on them!

Draw your magical box or container here!

Create a magical place you can visit in your mind, where you can release all your fears and take time to unwind. This place can be a castle, a garden, or even a fort! Whatever it is, it provides safety and support.

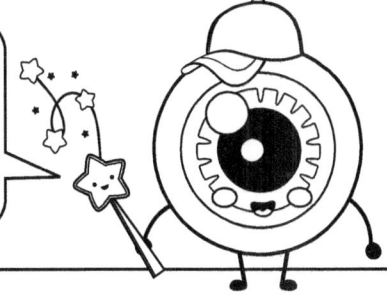

My Magical Place

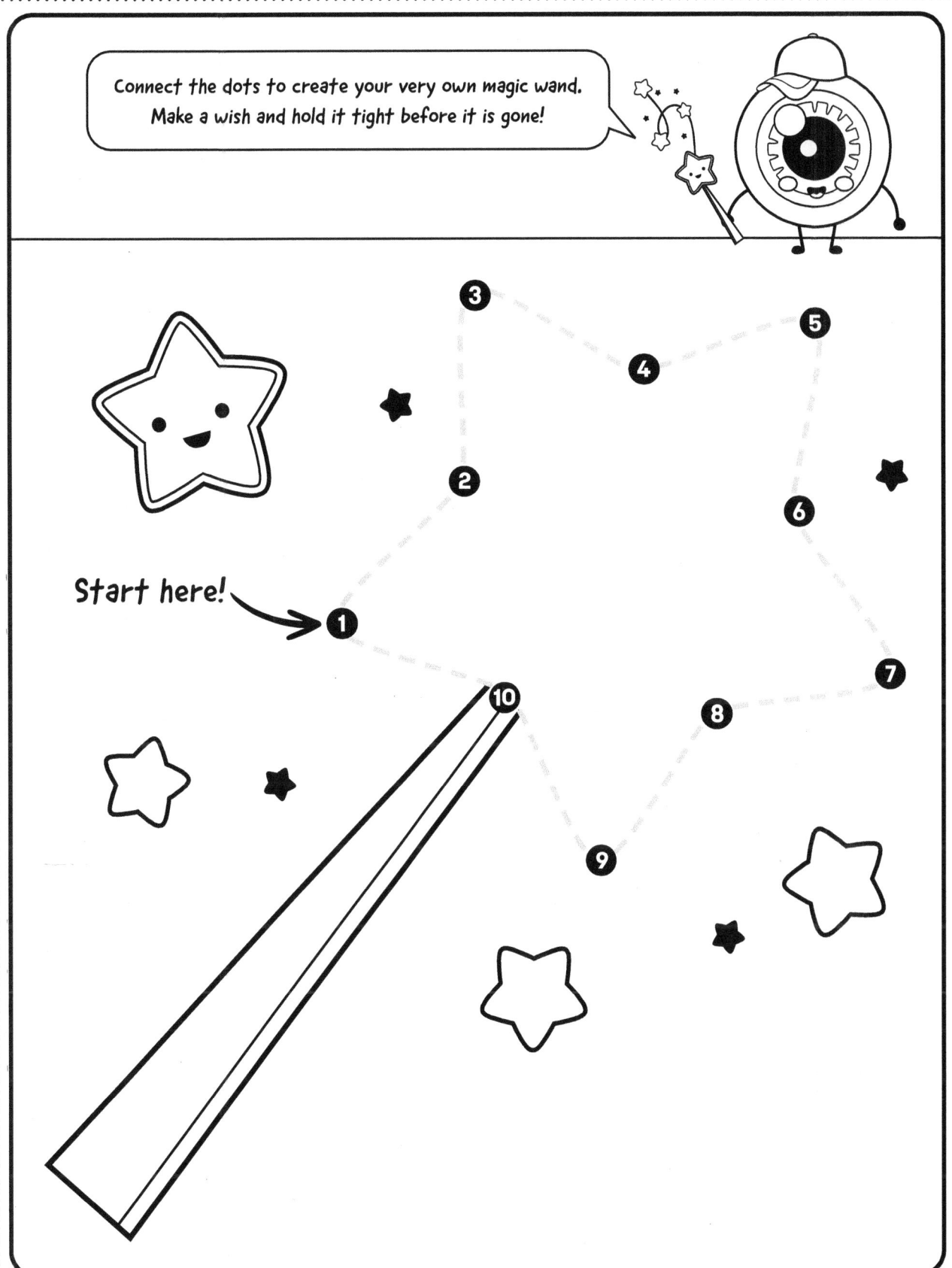

Can you inhale and exhale as you trace up and down, calming your body as you go all the way around?

Start here!

Breathe out → Breathe in ↗ Breathe out ↘ Breathe in → Breathe out ↙ Breathe in ← Breathe out ← Breathe in ↖ Breathe out ↑ Breathe in ↖

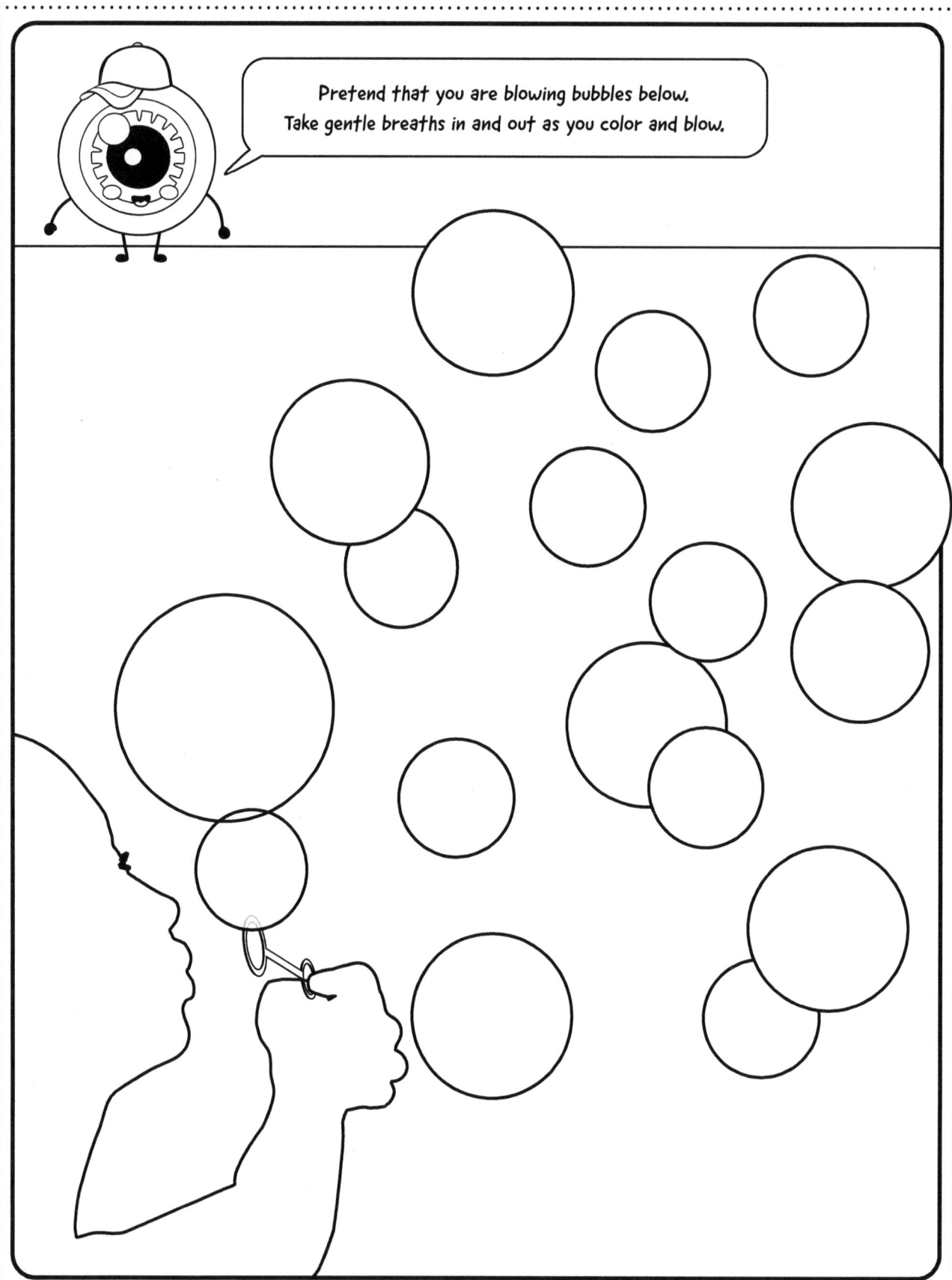

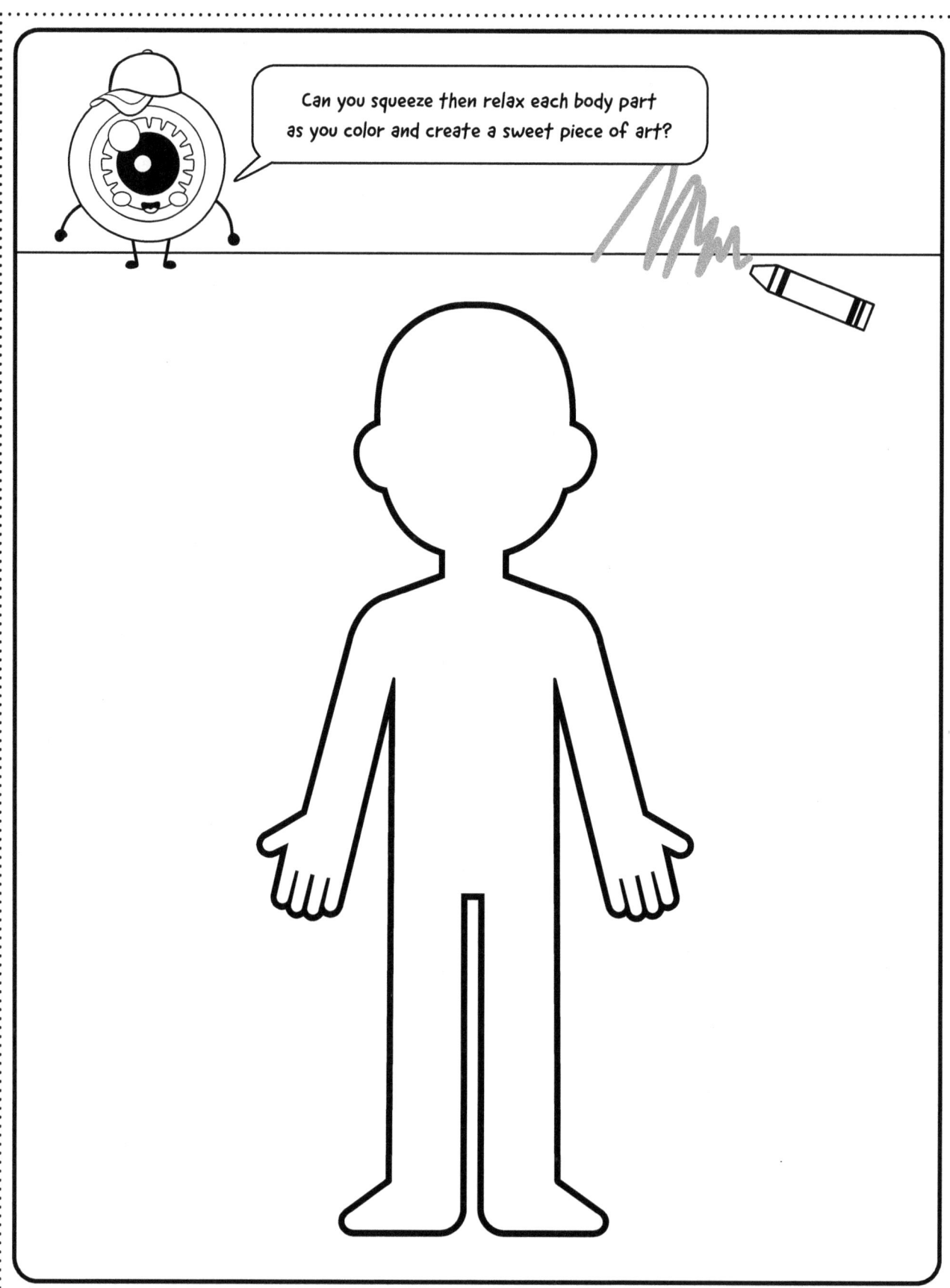

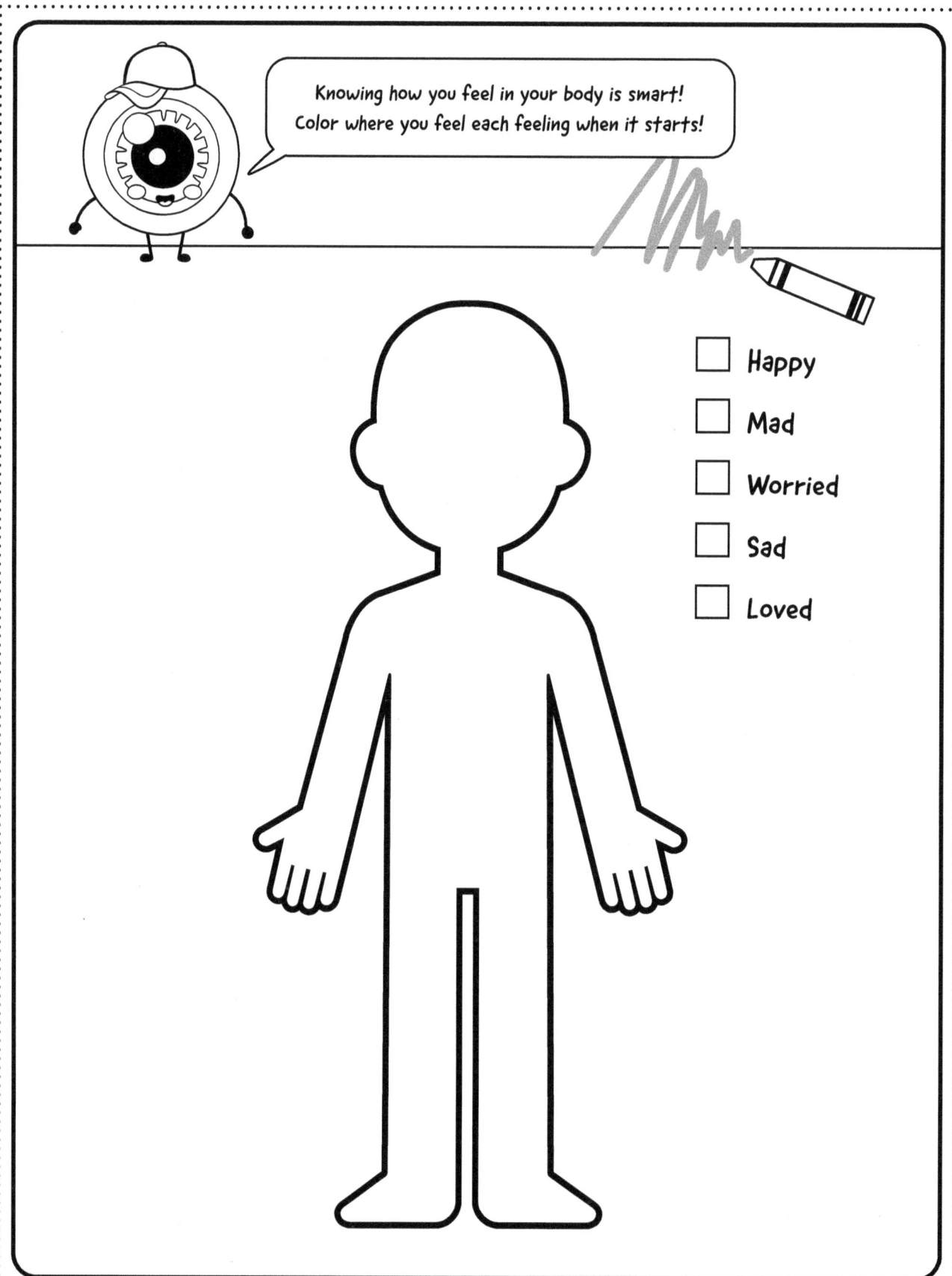

> Knowing your feelings is a huge superpower.
> Circle the ones that make you feel sour!

Worried

Mad

Scared

Sad

Confused

Happy

Embarrassed

Tired

Ashamed

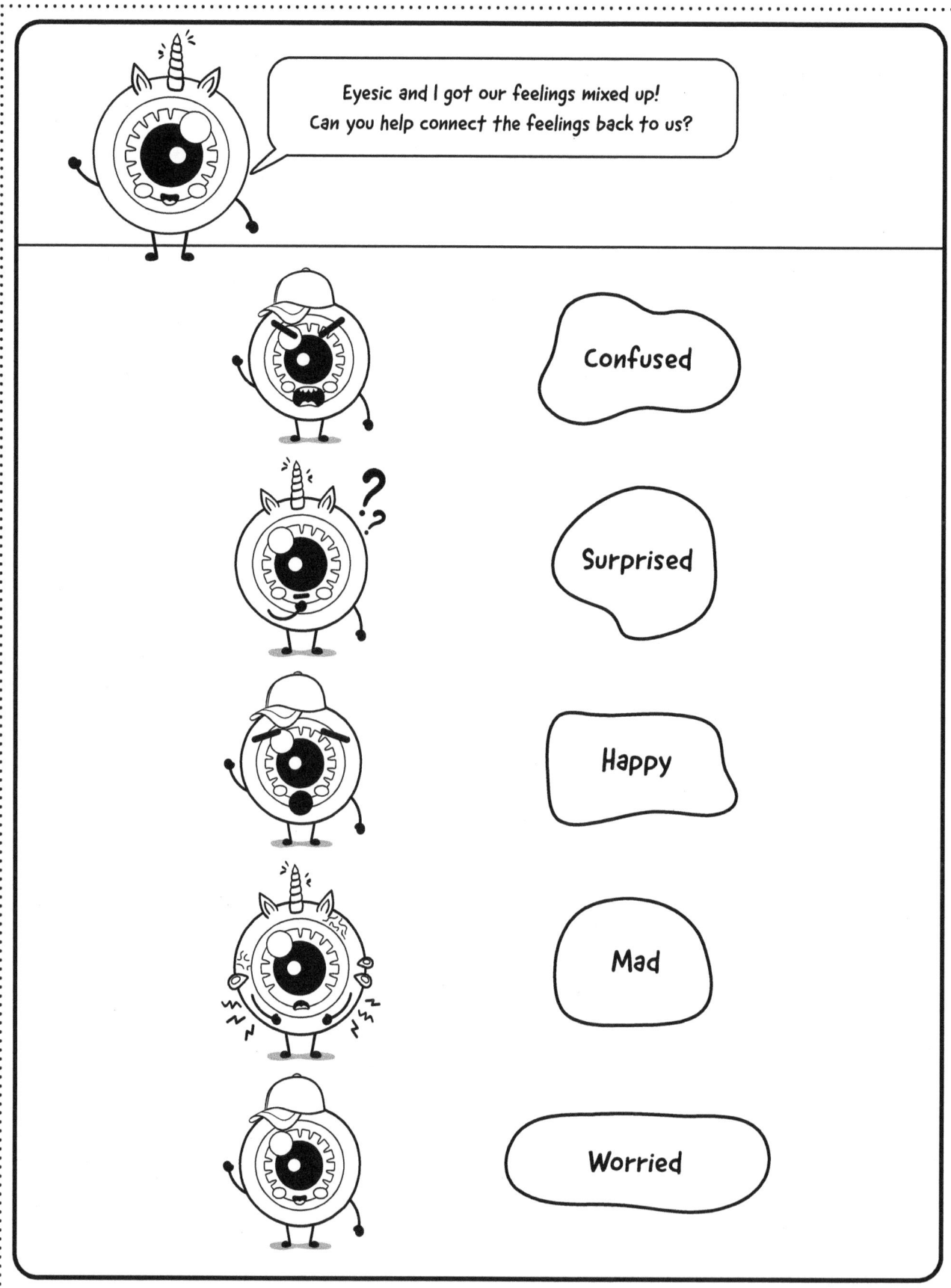

Let's learn a key part of how EMDR works, which involves moving back and forth!

Move your eyes side to side!

Tap your legs, shoulders, or knees back and forth!

Listen to music and move your body back and forth!

Moving back and forth helps your brain make sense of the scary things that happened and makes them feel less intense!

Here are some other ideas to move back and forth. We're wondering if you can come up with more!

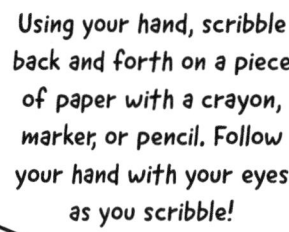

Using your hand, scribble back and forth on a piece of paper with a crayon, marker, or pencil. Follow your hand with your eyes as you scribble!

Pick your favorite song and do a dance move that has a back-and-forth motion! For example, shake your hips from side to side!

Use musical instruments such as drums or shakers to create back-and-forth movement.

Pick a part of your body to tap back and forth on! Try tapping your head, shoulders, knees, and toes!

Hula hoop using your hips and whole body to make back-and-forth movements.

Try a butterfly pose! Can you sit criss-cross applesauce and pretend that your legs are butterfly wings?

Pretend to be a tornado! Can you twist your body back and forth like a twister?

Pretend to be a rainbow! Can you use your arms to create a rainbow with your arms back and forth?

Shut Down

The other thing that happens when the stress is too much, is that Tolly gets really low and doesn't want to budge.

I'm tired.
I'm sad.
I'm checked out.

I'm hiding.
I'm avoiding.
I have low energy.

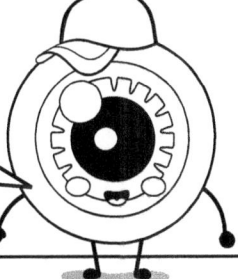

When he is feeling completely "shut down," he really does not want anyone around.

Circle the Tolly that you might feel when you are faced with a situation that isn't ideal.

	In the Zone	Out of Control	Shut Down
 You are hungry but it will be a while until you can grab some food to eat!		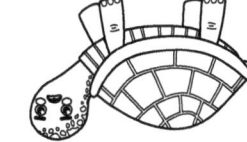	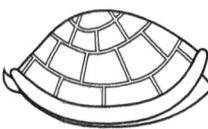
 You work really hard on something but you still don't get it right.		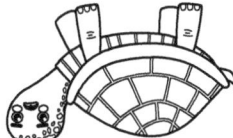	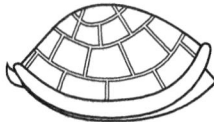
 Your friends think that you have a good idea!		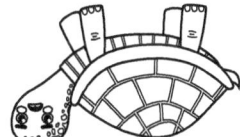	
 Your teacher asks you to answer a question in front of the class.		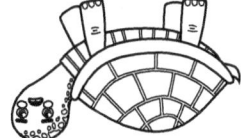	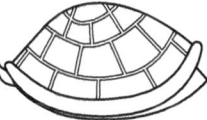
 You get to listen to your favorite song.			

Below are some thoughts that are pretty helpful. Color the hearts that make you feel grateful!

- ♡ I am good.
- ♡ I am beautiful.
- ♡ I am kind.
- ♡ I am smart.
- ♡ I am enough.
- ♡ I am worthy.
- ♡ I belong.
- ♡ I can handle it.
- ♡ I am different, in a good way.
- ♡ I am safe.
- ♡ I can have big emotions.
- ♡ I can ask for help.
- ♡ I am learning.
- ♡ I can learn.
- ♡ It is okay to make mistakes.
- ♡ I did my best.
- ♡ I can do it.
- ♡ I can try my best.
- ♡ I matter.
- ♡ I am wonderful.

Sometimes, kind words don't truly feel real. Can you rate and color how true these words feel?

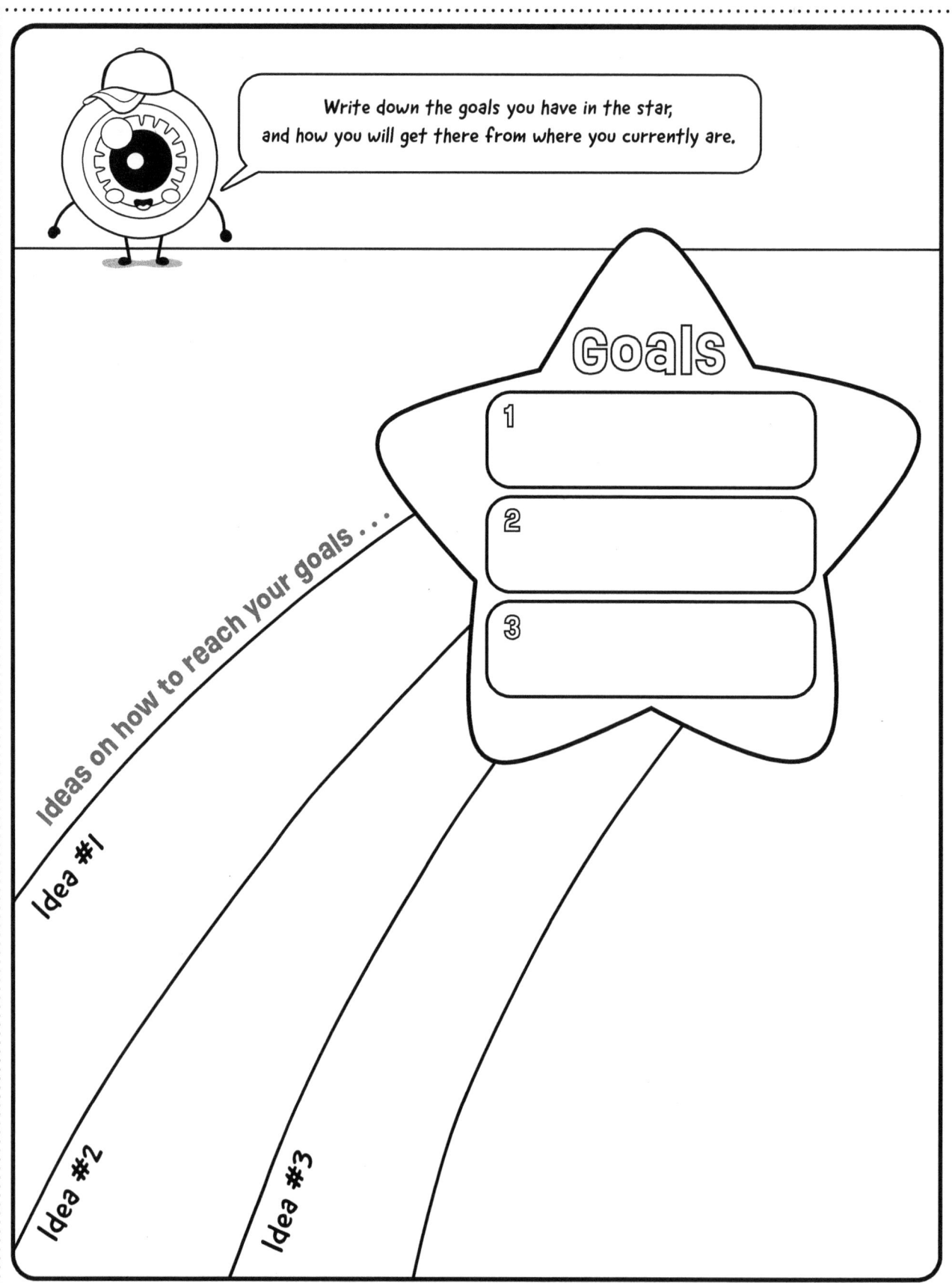

What you know in your mind doesn't always match your body and heart. You may know it's true in your head, but it feels false in other parts. It takes time and practice to sort it all through. Can you help Brainy match a few?

My Mind → **My Heart** → **My Body**

My Mind	My Heart	My Body
✓ I can do it!	✗ Sad and worried	✗ Stomachache
✓ I can do it!	✓ Excited and determined	✓ Fuzzy feeling in my heart
○ I am proud.	○ Scared	○ Racing heartbeat
○ I am proud.	○ Happy	○ Relaxed

Eyela is having trouble with bad thoughts in her head. Can you help find good thoughts for her instead?

Search for Good Thoughts

```
E I J A X I M O Y L U F P L E H
Y O P I W V L P H E B A J O R Z
E L V N C E K O M X S Q U V I E
S Q T E E W S N U M Y A M E C W
I K Y X G N I O L G K I N D F Y
C E A D R B Z A M H P L A H X P
E V I T A E R C D E Q N I S O P
L U O Z Y F X L A J U E Y E L A
Z F H P A T I E N T B T F E A H
B R E M I O F M R R E A N G K Y
V I G Y K L E A U Q S L O Z O X
J E I N Z U M J I D F E V A R B
G N M A K S Q O S K W N P S G A
E D N D A O P D A Z O T C O J N
A L U E R C Y T F I J E X L U I
W Y L L I S Q N E B C D E F R Z
```

I am... ???

Awesome	Fun	Loved	Smart
Brave	Happy	Patient	Sweet
Creative	Helpful	Safe	Talented
Friendly	Kind	Silly	

Answers: Look on page 105.

> When the problems get too big to take, use your stop sign to take a break! Decorate your EMDR stop sign here and use it when you wish, my dear!

STOP

Activating Problem #1

Step 2

When you think about your 🎯 target problem, what is the unhealthy thought you store? Choose one from below or create some more!

- ☐ I am bad.
- ☐ I am ugly.
- ☐ I am mean.
- ☐ I'm not smart.
- ☐ I'm not enough.
- ☐ I am worthless.
- ☐ I don't belong.
- ☐ I can't handle it.
- ☐ I am different.
- ☐ I'm not safe.
- ☐ Create your own: _____
- ☐ Create your own: _____

- ☐ I am angry.
- ☐ I can't ask for help.
- ☐ I am dumb.
- ☐ I can't learn.
- ☐ I always mess up.
- ☐ It is my fault.
- ☐ I can't do it.
- ☐ I am the worst.
- ☐ I don't matter.
- ☐ I need to be perfect.
- ☐ Create your own: _____
- ☐ Create your own: _____

Activating Problem #1

Step 3

When you think about your target problem, what is the healthy thought you want instead? Circle the one that you want to keep in your head.

- ♡ I am good.
- ♡ I am beautiful.
- ♡ I am kind.
- ♡ I am smart.
- ♡ I am enough.
- ♡ I am worthy.
- ♡ I belong.
- ♡ I can handle it.
- ♡ I am different, in a good way.
- ♡ I am safe.
- ♡ Create your own: _____
- ♡ Create your own: _____

- ♡ I can have big emotions.
- ♡ I can ask for help.
- ♡ I am learning.
- ♡ I can learn.
- ♡ It is okay to make mistakes.
- ♡ I did my best.
- ♡ I can do it.
- ♡ I can try my best.
- ♡ I matter.
- ♡ I am wonderful.
- ♡ Create your own: _____
- ♡ Create your own: _____

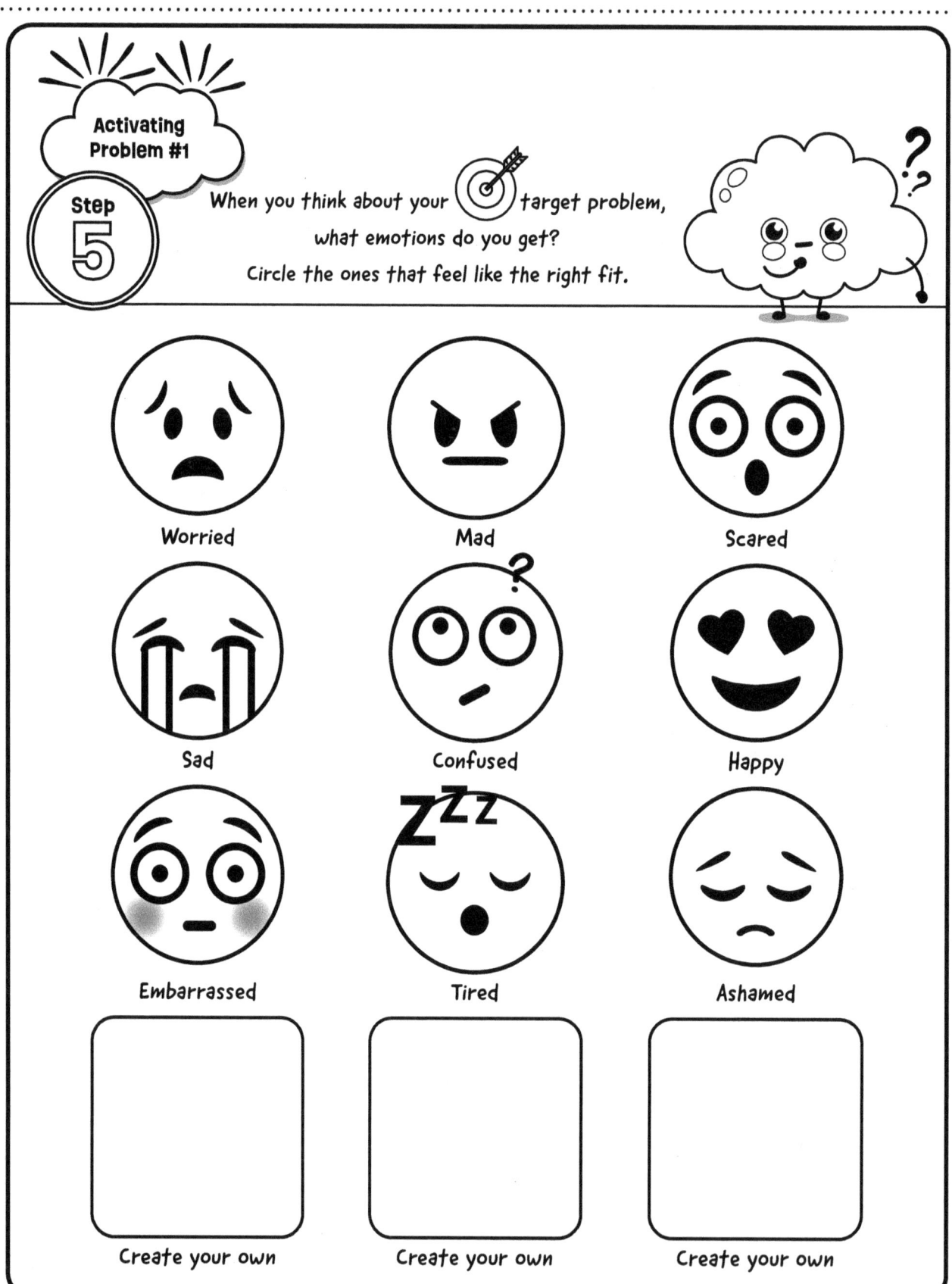

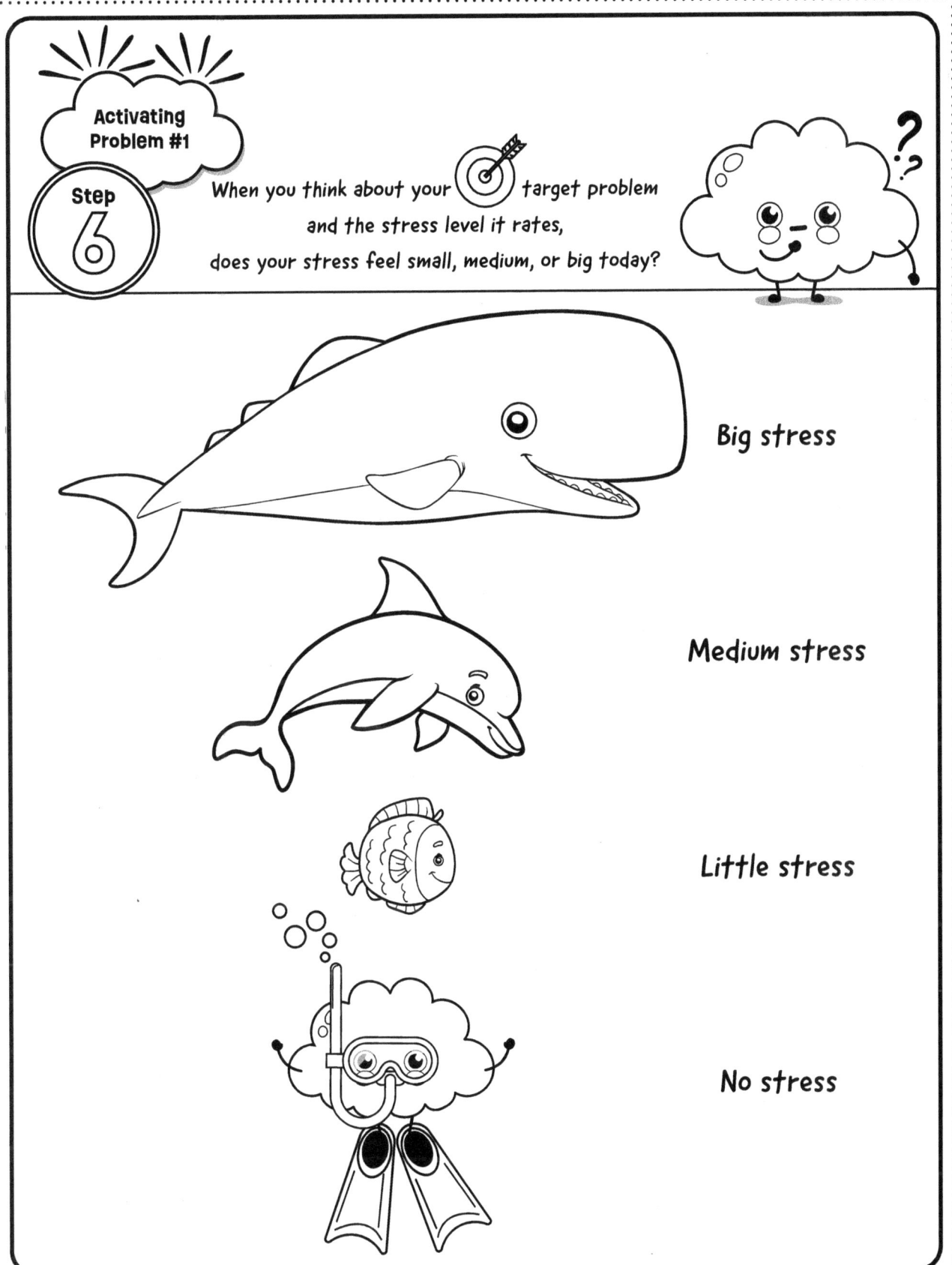

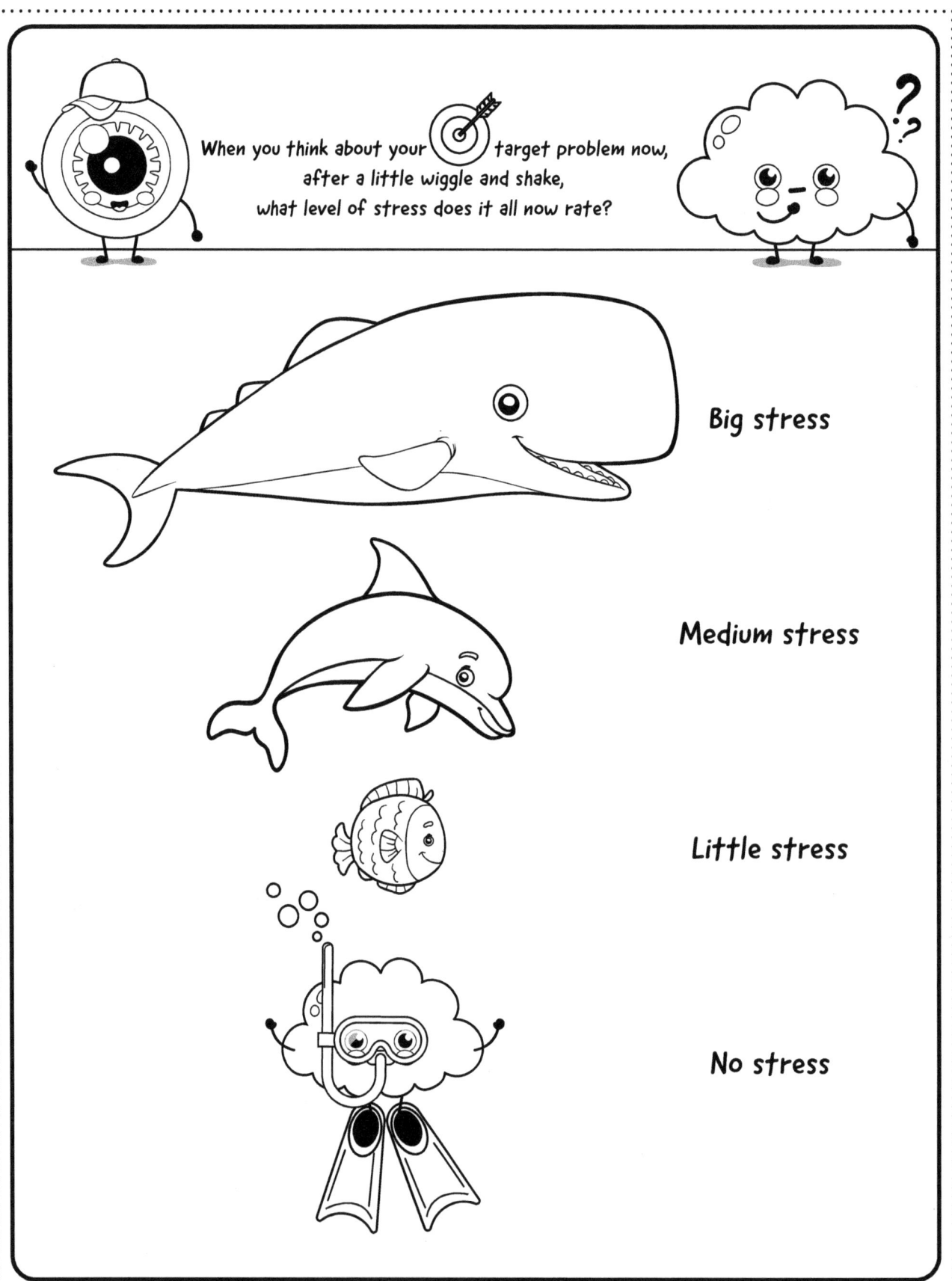

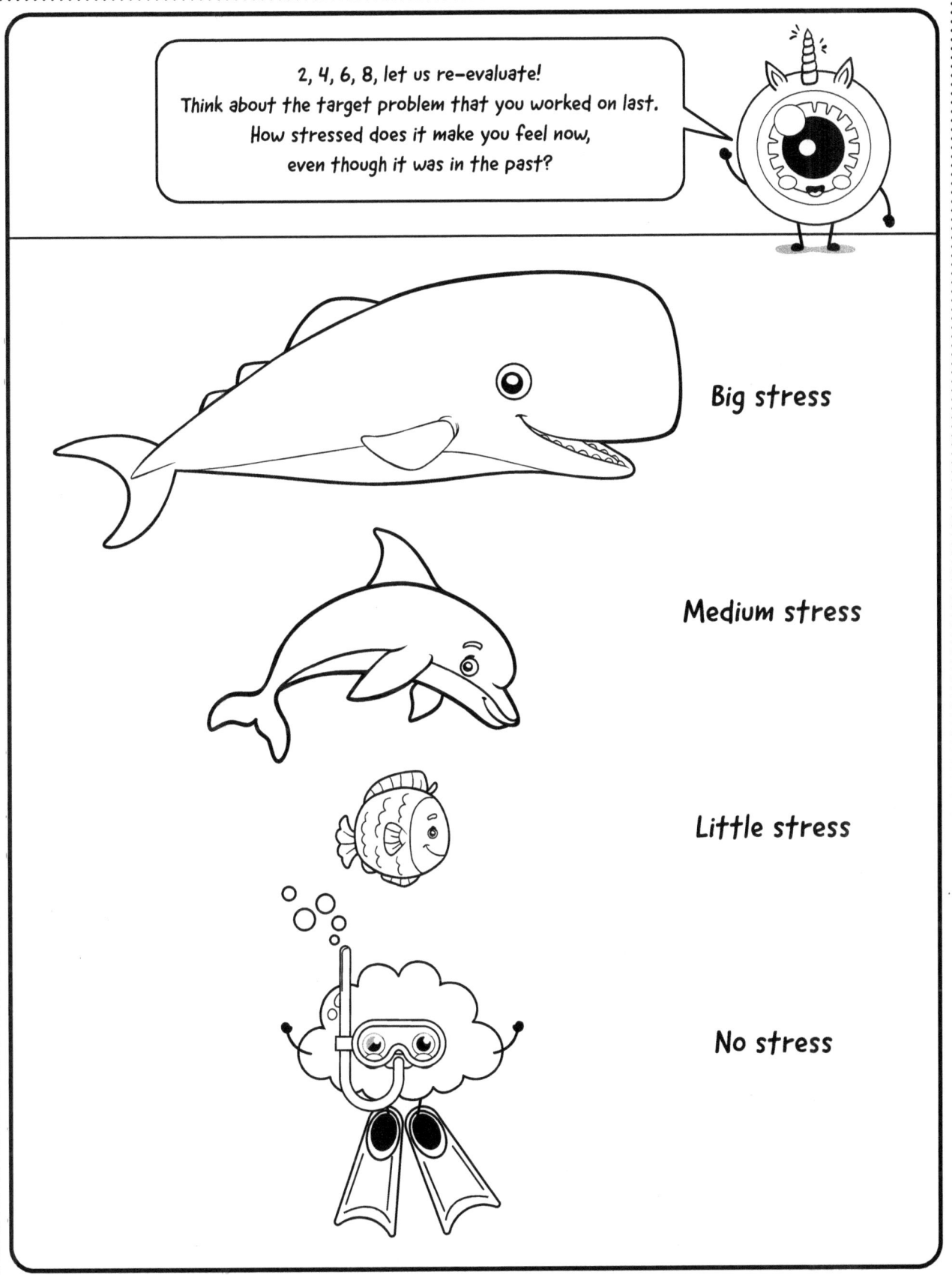

After working through the last target problem, were there any changes you noticed? Perhaps things felt much easier, or maybe you found it harder to focus. There is no right or wrong answer, as every problem is unique! Check the boxes that happened to you in the last week!

- ☐ New thoughts
- ☐ New feelings
- ☐ New dreams
- ☐ New memories
- ☐ New body feelings
- ☐ Nothing much
- ☐ Feeling happier
- ☐ Feeling normal
- ☐ Feeling the same
- ☐ Feeling scared
- ☐ More nightmares
- ☐ Fewer nightmares

- ☐ Feeling worse
- ☐ Feeling better
- ☐ Blaming myself or others
- ☐ Isolating
- ☐ Trouble sleeping
- ☐ Having more focus
- ☐ Having less focus
- ☐ Being clingy
- ☐ Create your own: _____
- ☐ Create your own: _____

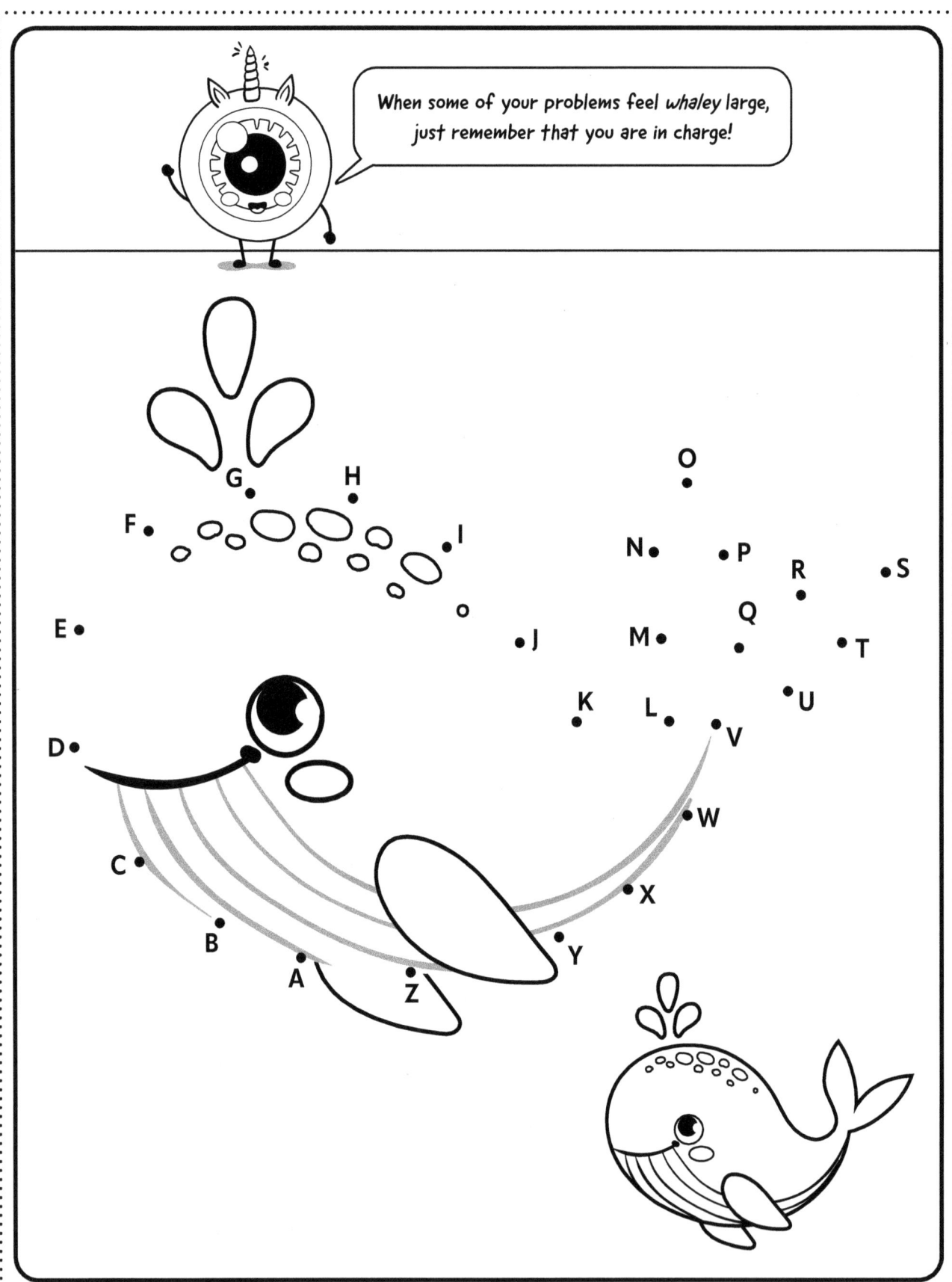

Activating Problem #2

Step 2

When you think about your 🎯 target problem, what is the unhealthy thought you store? Choose one from below or create some more!

HELP!

- ☐ I am bad.
- ☐ I am ugly.
- ☐ I am mean.
- ☐ I'm not smart.
- ☐ I'm not enough.
- ☐ I am worthless.
- ☐ I don't belong.
- ☐ I can't handle it.
- ☐ I am different.
- ☐ I'm not safe.
- ☐ Create your own: _____
- ☐ Create your own: _____

- ☐ I am angry.
- ☐ I can't ask for help.
- ☐ I am dumb.
- ☐ I can't learn.
- ☐ I always mess up.
- ☐ It is my fault.
- ☐ I can't do it.
- ☐ I am the worst.
- ☐ I don't matter.
- ☐ I need to be perfect.
- ☐ Create your own: _____
- ☐ Create your own: _____

Activating Problem #2

Step 3

When you think about your 🎯 target problem, what is the healthy thought you want instead? Circle the one that you want to keep in your head.

HELP!

- ♡ I am good.
- ♡ I am beautiful.
- ♡ I am kind.
- ♡ I am smart.
- ♡ I am enough.
- ♡ I am worthy.
- ♡ I belong.
- ♡ I can handle it.
- ♡ I am different, in a good way.
- ♡ I am safe.
- ♡ Create your own: _____
- ♡ Create your own: _____

- ♡ I can have big emotions.
- ♡ I can ask for help.
- ♡ I am learning.
- ♡ I can learn.
- ♡ It is okay to make mistakes.
- ♡ I did my best.
- ♡ I can do it.
- ♡ I can try my best.
- ♡ I matter.
- ♡ I am wonderful.
- ♡ Create your own: _____
- ♡ Create your own: _____

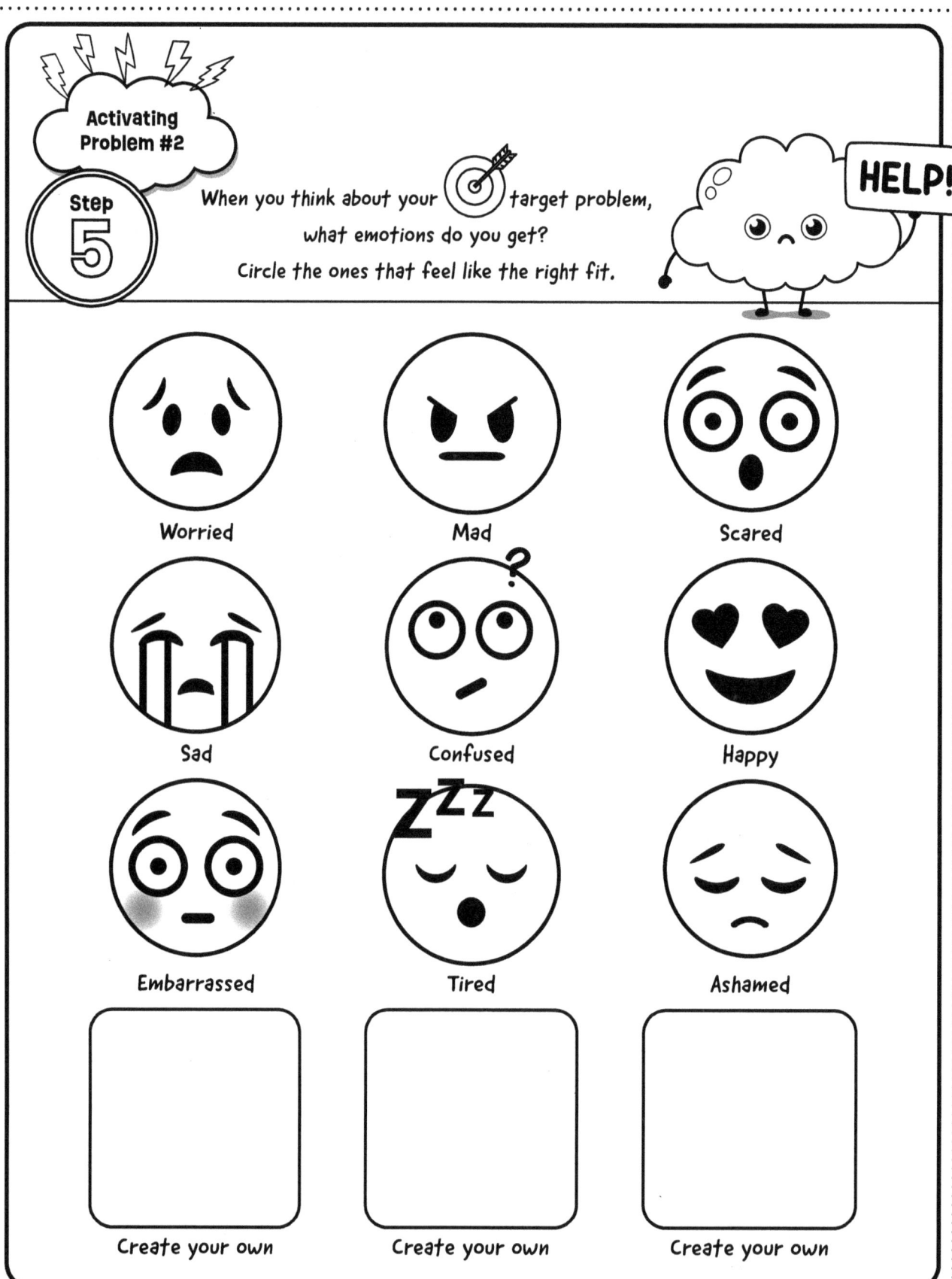

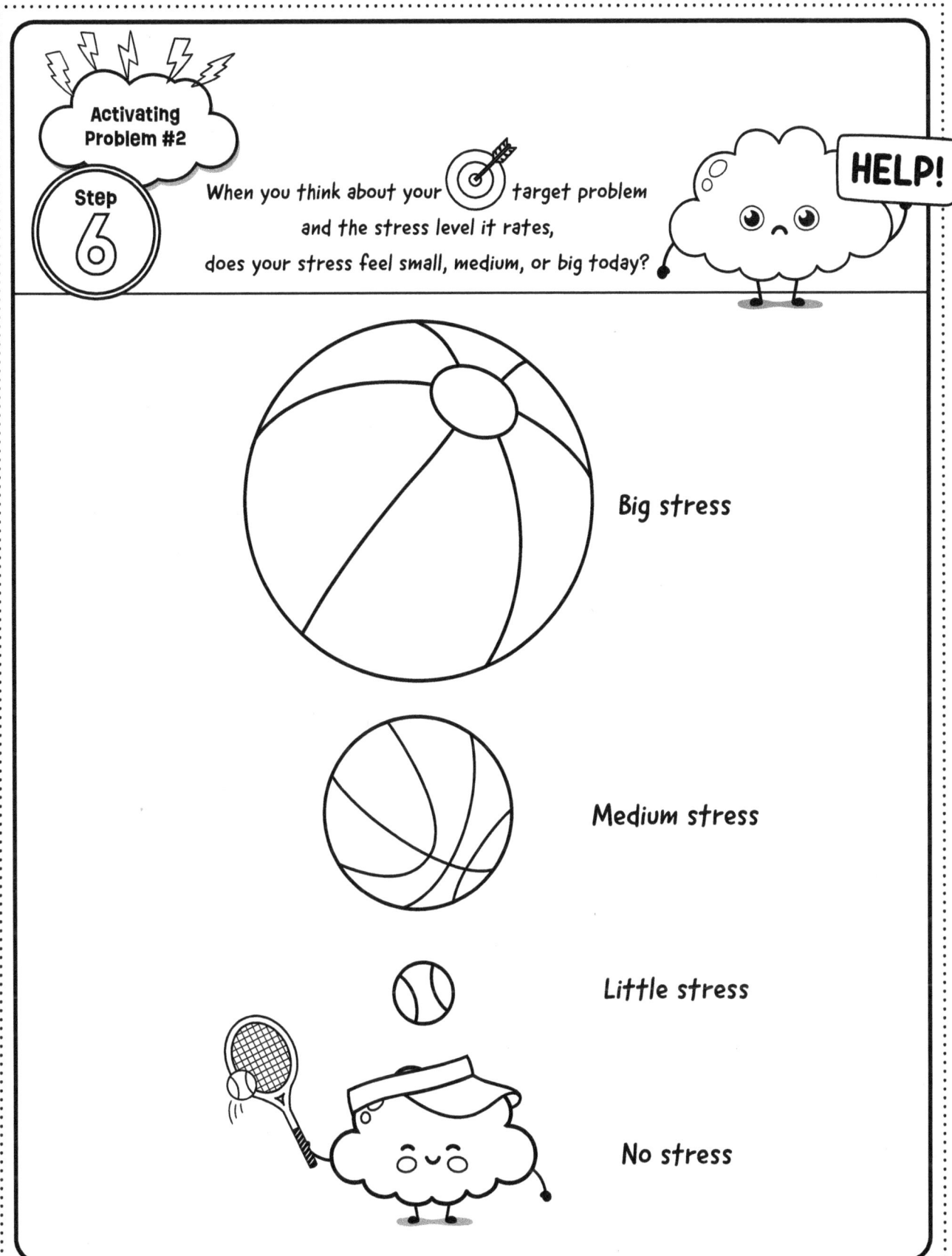

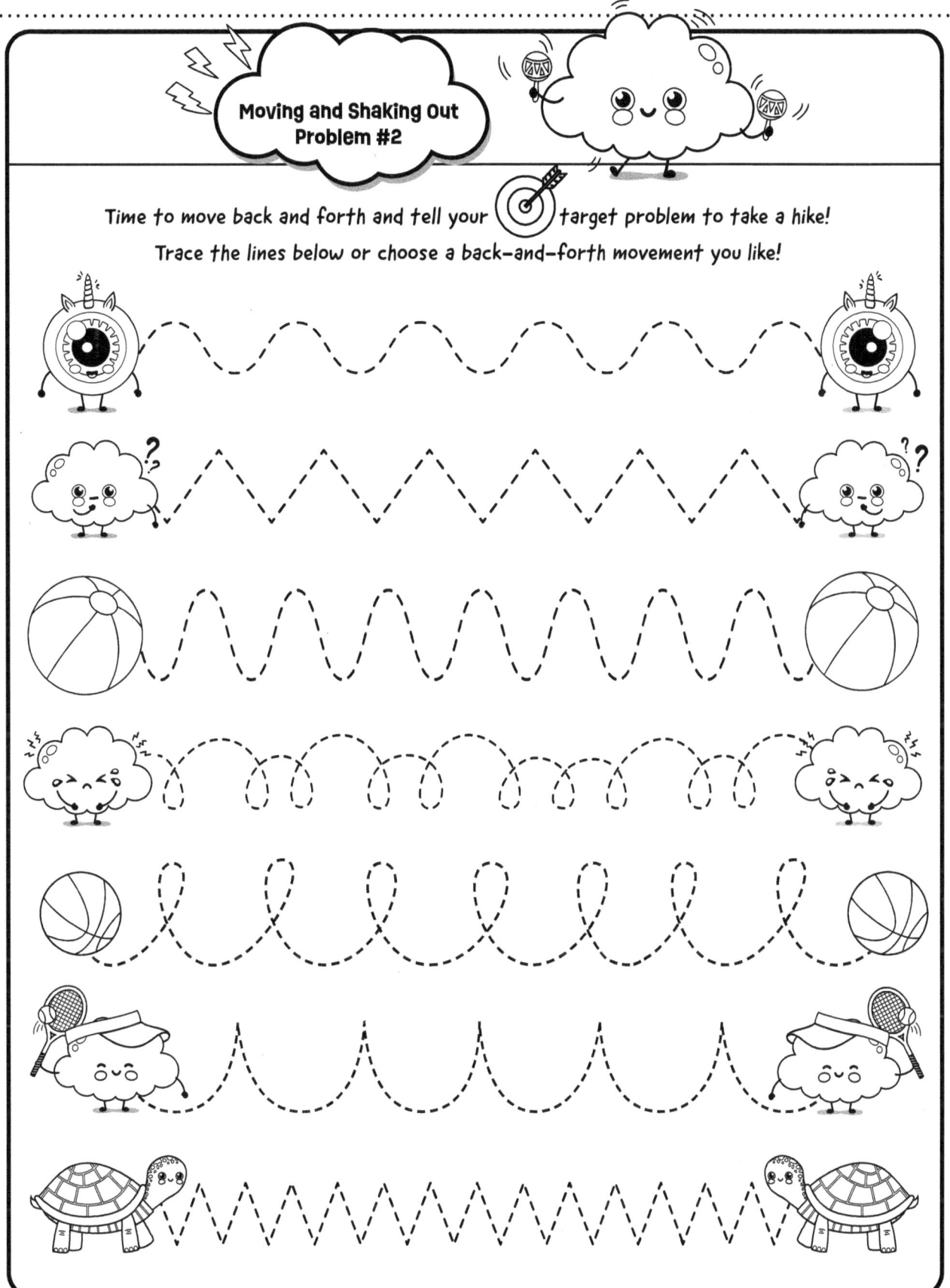

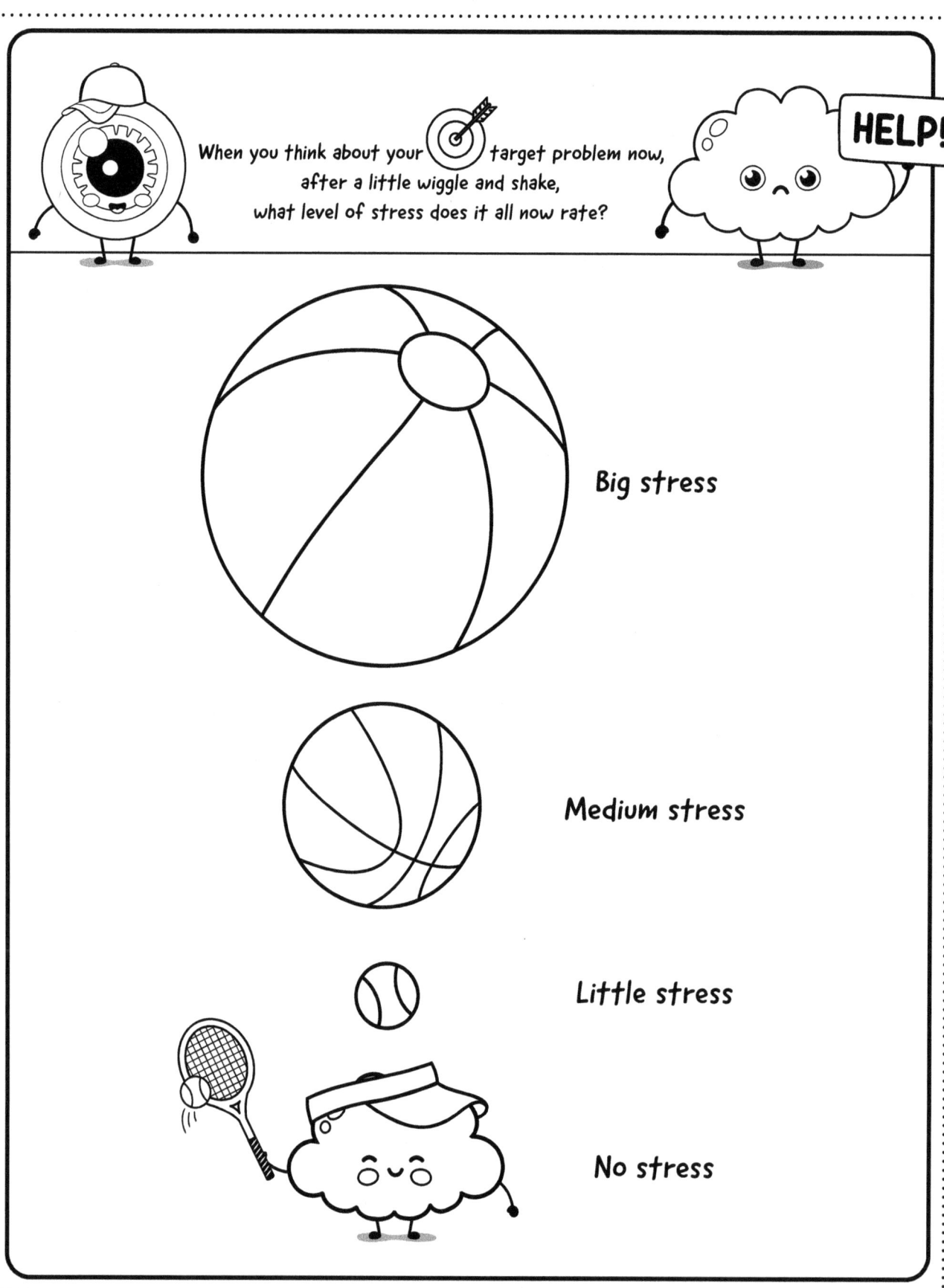

2, 4, 6, 8, let us re-evaluate!
Think about the target problem that you worked on last.
How stressed does it make you feel now,
even though it was in the past?

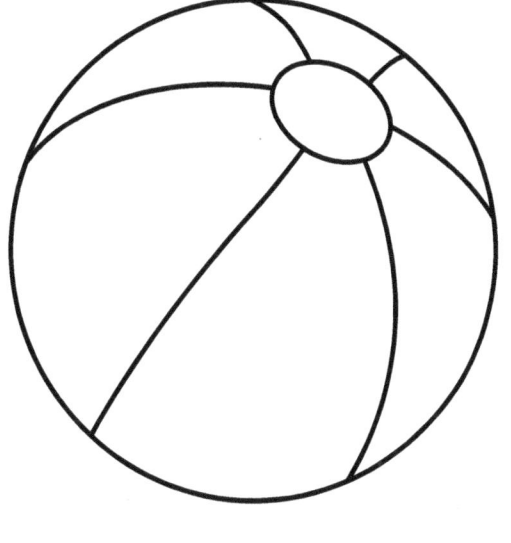 Big stress

 Medium stress

Little stress

 No stress

After working through the last target problem, were there any changes you noticed? Perhaps things felt much easier, or maybe you found it harder to focus. There is no right or wrong answer, as every problem is unique! Check the boxes that happened to you in the last week!

- ☐ New thoughts
- ☐ New feelings
- ☐ New dreams
- ☐ New memories
- ☐ New body feelings
- ☐ Nothing much
- ☐ Feeling happier
- ☐ Feeling normal
- ☐ Feeling the same
- ☐ Feeling scared
- ☐ More nightmares
- ☐ Fewer nightmares

- ☐ Feeling worse
- ☐ Feeling better
- ☐ Blaming myself or others
- ☐ Isolating
- ☐ Trouble sleeping
- ☐ Having more focus
- ☐ Having less focus
- ☐ Being clingy
- ☐ Create your own:
  _____
- ☐ Create your own:
  _____

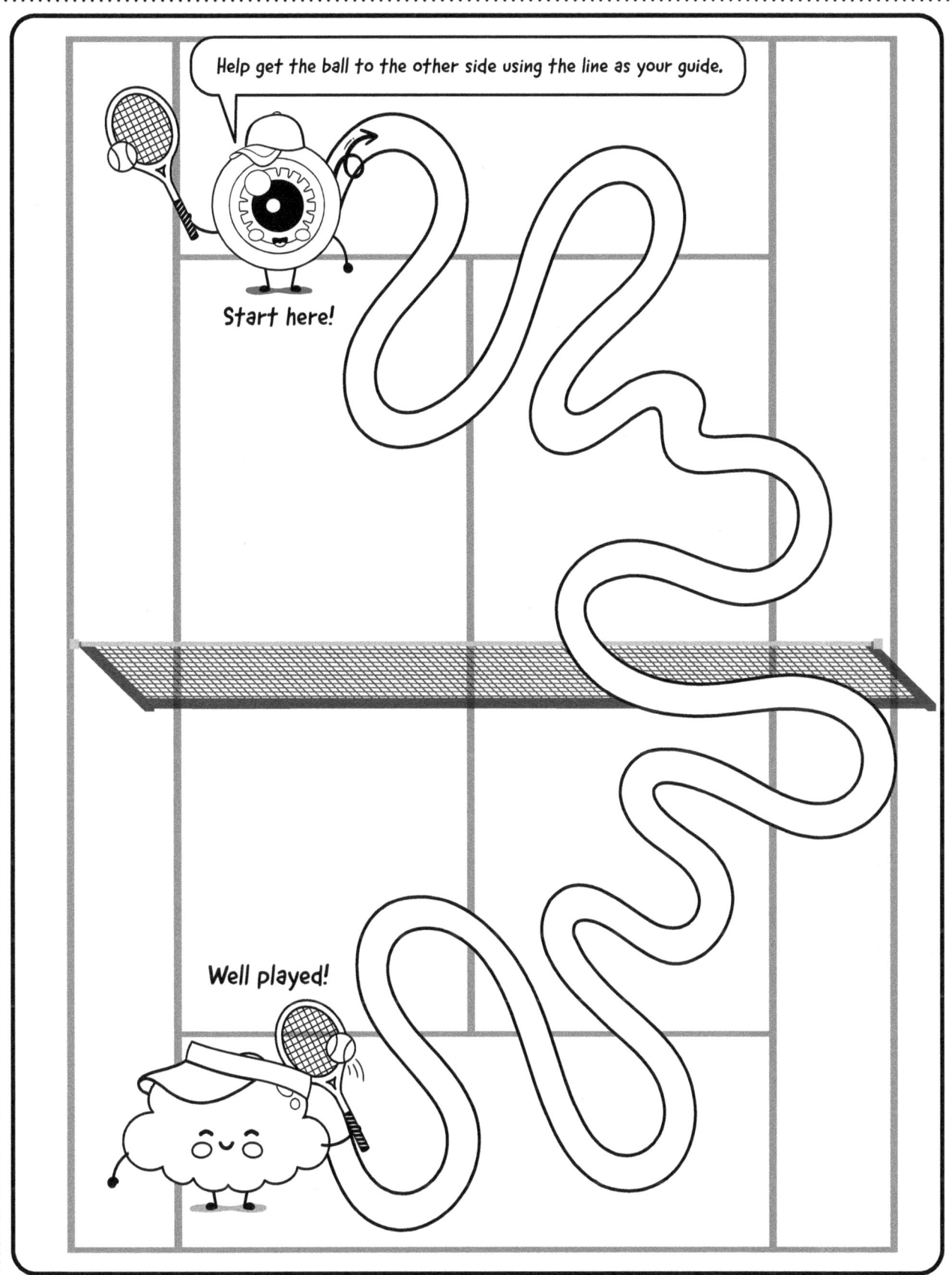

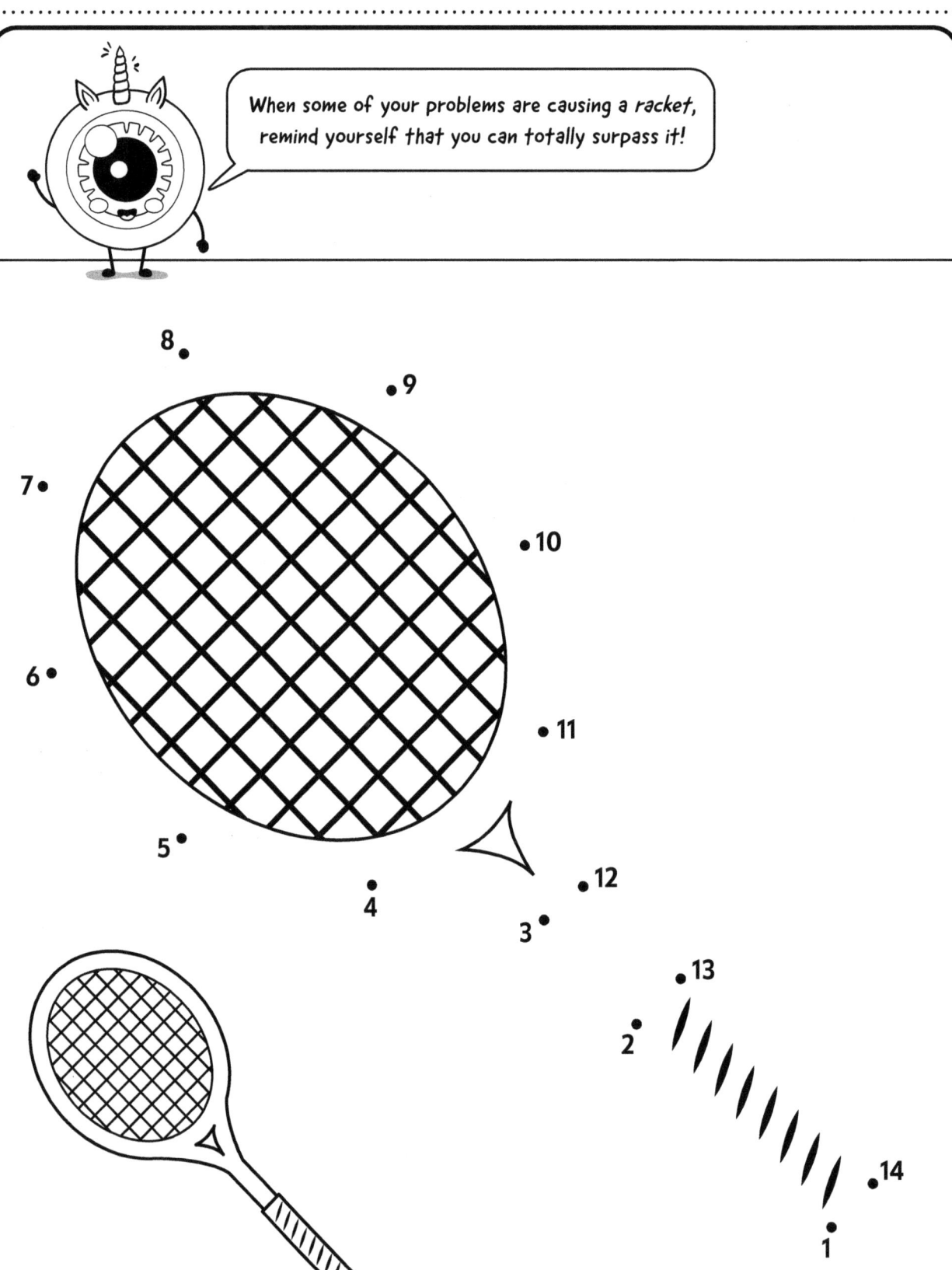

Activating Problem #3

Step 2

When you think about your 🎯 target problem, what is the unhealthy thought you store? Choose one from below or create some more!

- ☐ I am bad.
- ☐ I am ugly.
- ☐ I am mean.
- ☐ I'm not smart.
- ☐ I'm not enough.
- ☐ I am worthless.
- ☐ I don't belong.
- ☐ I can't handle it.
- ☐ I am different.
- ☐ I'm not safe.
- ☐ Create your own: _____
- ☐ Create your own: _____

- ☐ I am angry.
- ☐ I can't ask for help.
- ☐ I am dumb.
- ☐ I can't learn.
- ☐ I always mess up.
- ☐ It is my fault.
- ☐ I can't do it.
- ☐ I am the worst.
- ☐ I don't matter.
- ☐ I need to be perfect.
- ☐ Create your own: _____
- ☐ Create your own: _____

Activating Problem #3

Step 3

When you think about your target problem, what is the healthy thought you want instead? Circle the one that you want to keep in your head.

- ♡ I am good.
- ♡ I am beautiful.
- ♡ I am kind.
- ♡ I am smart.
- ♡ I am enough.
- ♡ I am worthy.
- ♡ I belong.
- ♡ I can handle it.
- ♡ I am different, in a good way.
- ♡ I am safe.
- ♡ Create your own: _____
- ♡ Create your own: _____

- ♡ I can have big emotions.
- ♡ I can ask for help.
- ♡ I am learning.
- ♡ I can learn.
- ♡ It is okay to make mistakes.
- ♡ I did my best.
- ♡ I can do it.
- ♡ I can try my best.
- ♡ I matter.
- ♡ I am wonderful.
- ♡ Create your own: _____
- ♡ Create your own: _____

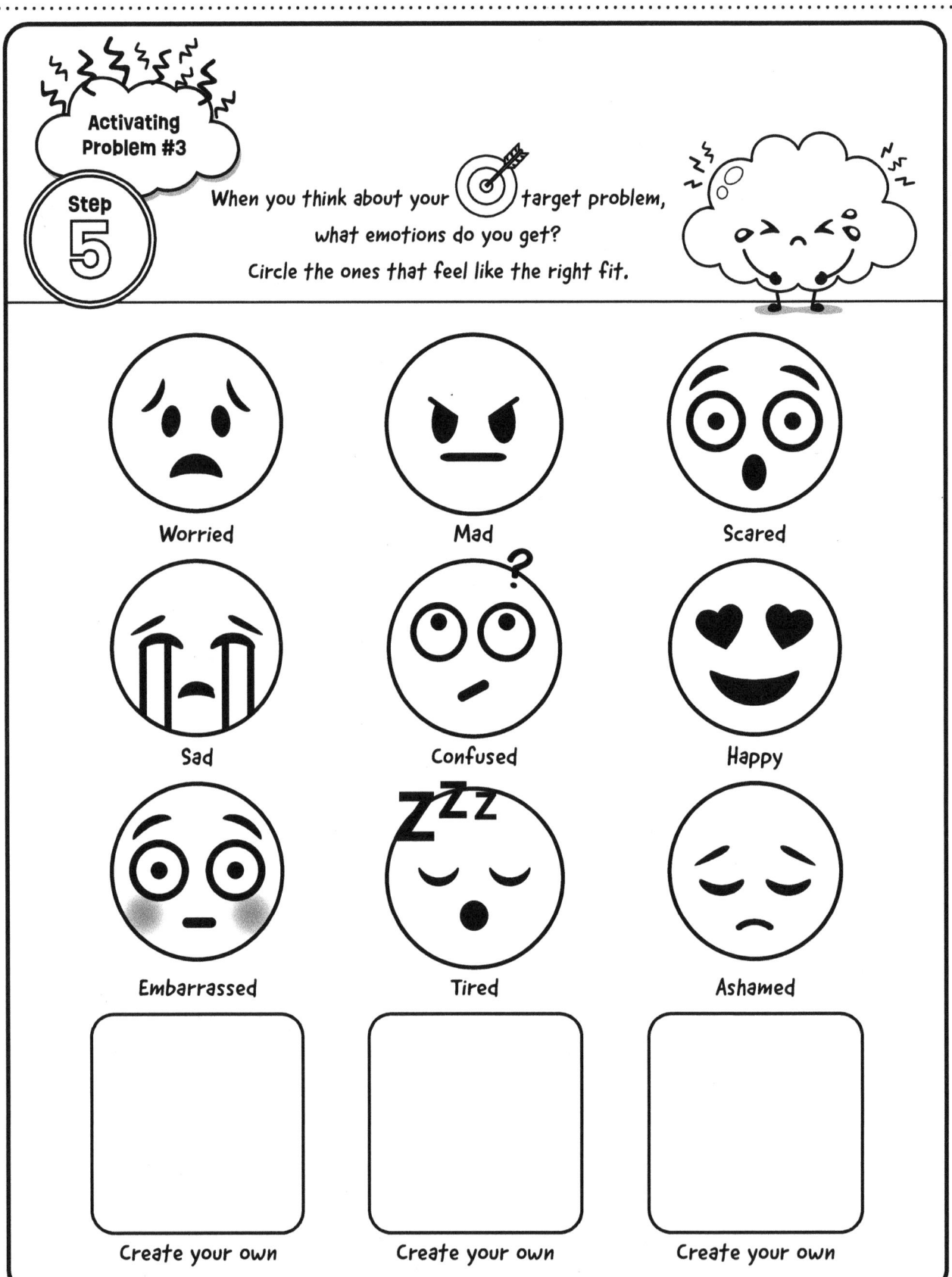

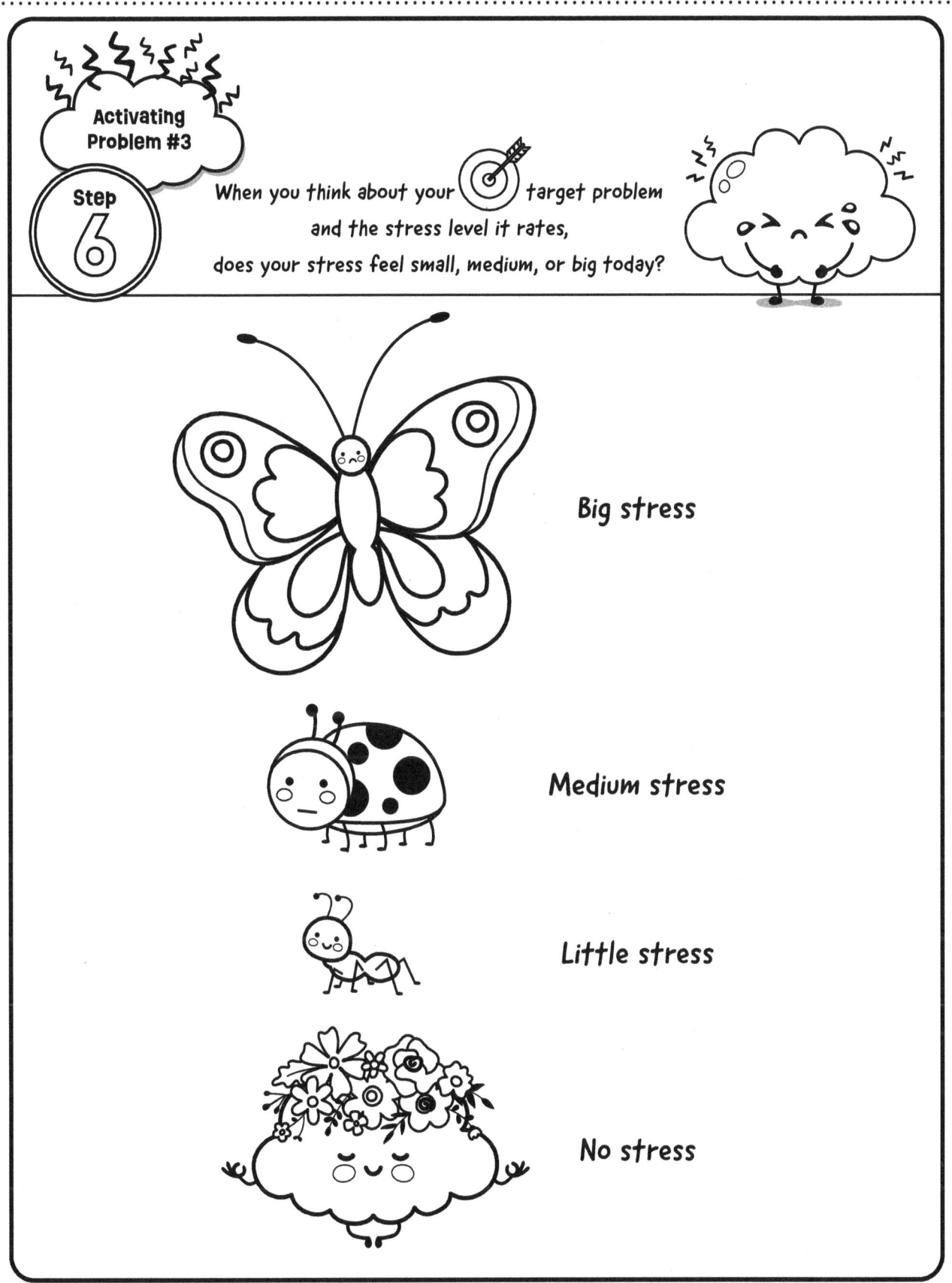

 When you think about your  target problem now, after a little wiggle and shake, what level of stress does it all now rate?

 Big stress

 Medium stress

 Little stress

 No stress

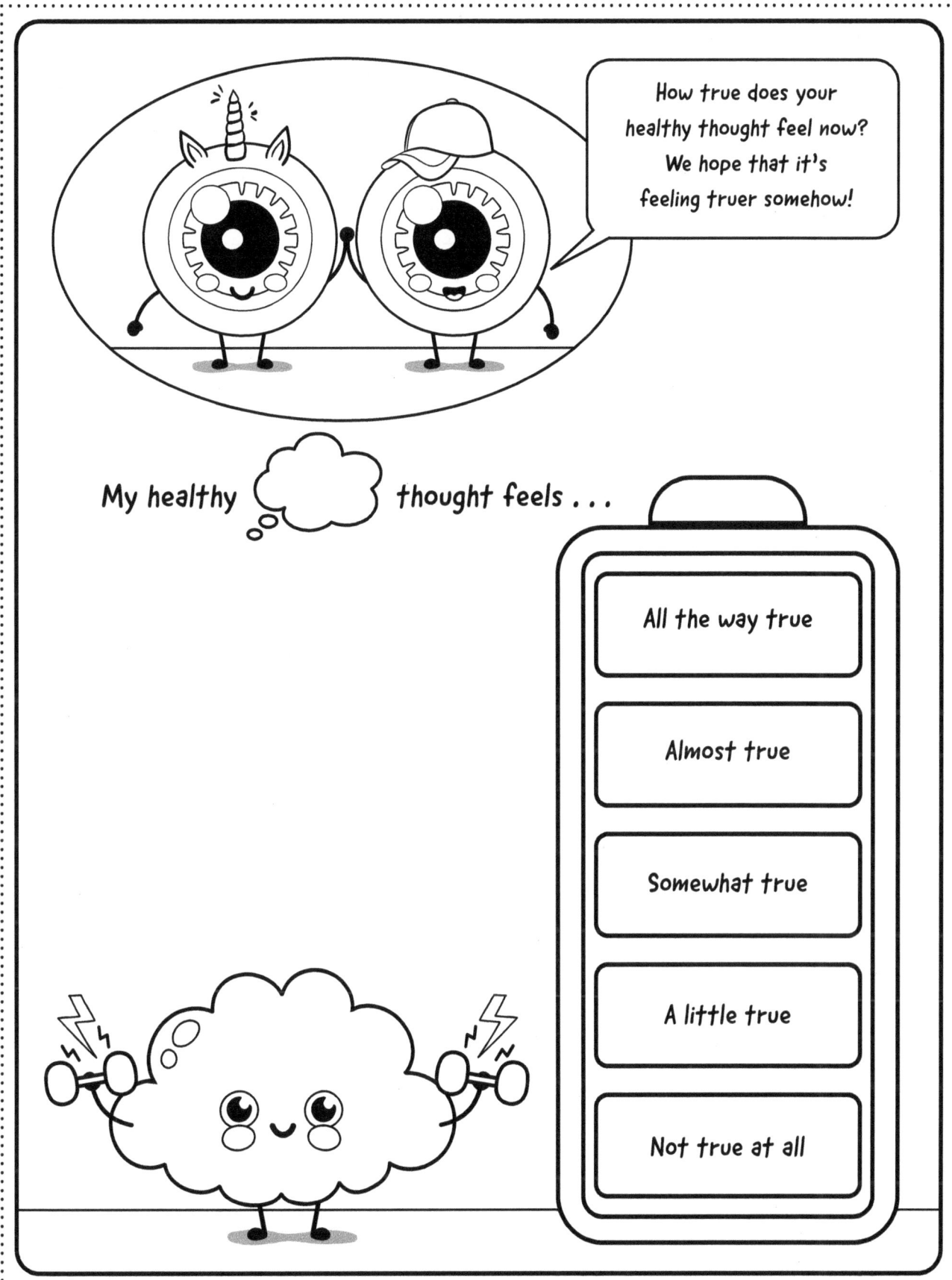

2, 4, 6, 8, let us re-evaluate!
Think about the target problem that you worked on last.
How stressed does it make you feel now,
even though it was in the past?

   Big stress

   Medium stress

   Little stress

   No stress

After working through the last target problem, were there any changes you noticed? Perhaps things felt much easier, or maybe you found it harder to focus. There is no right or wrong answer, as every problem is unique! Check the boxes that happened to you in the last week!

- ☐ New thoughts
- ☐ New feelings
- ☐ New dreams
- ☐ New memories
- ☐ New body feelings
- ☐ Nothing much
- ☐ Feeling happier
- ☐ Feeling normal
- ☐ Feeling the same
- ☐ Feeling scared
- ☐ More nightmares
- ☐ Fewer nightmares

- ☐ Feeling worse
- ☐ Feeling better
- ☐ Blaming myself or others
- ☐ Isolating
- ☐ Trouble sleeping
- ☐ Having more focus
- ☐ Having less focus
- ☐ Being clingy
- ☐ Create your own: _____
- ☐ Create your own: _____

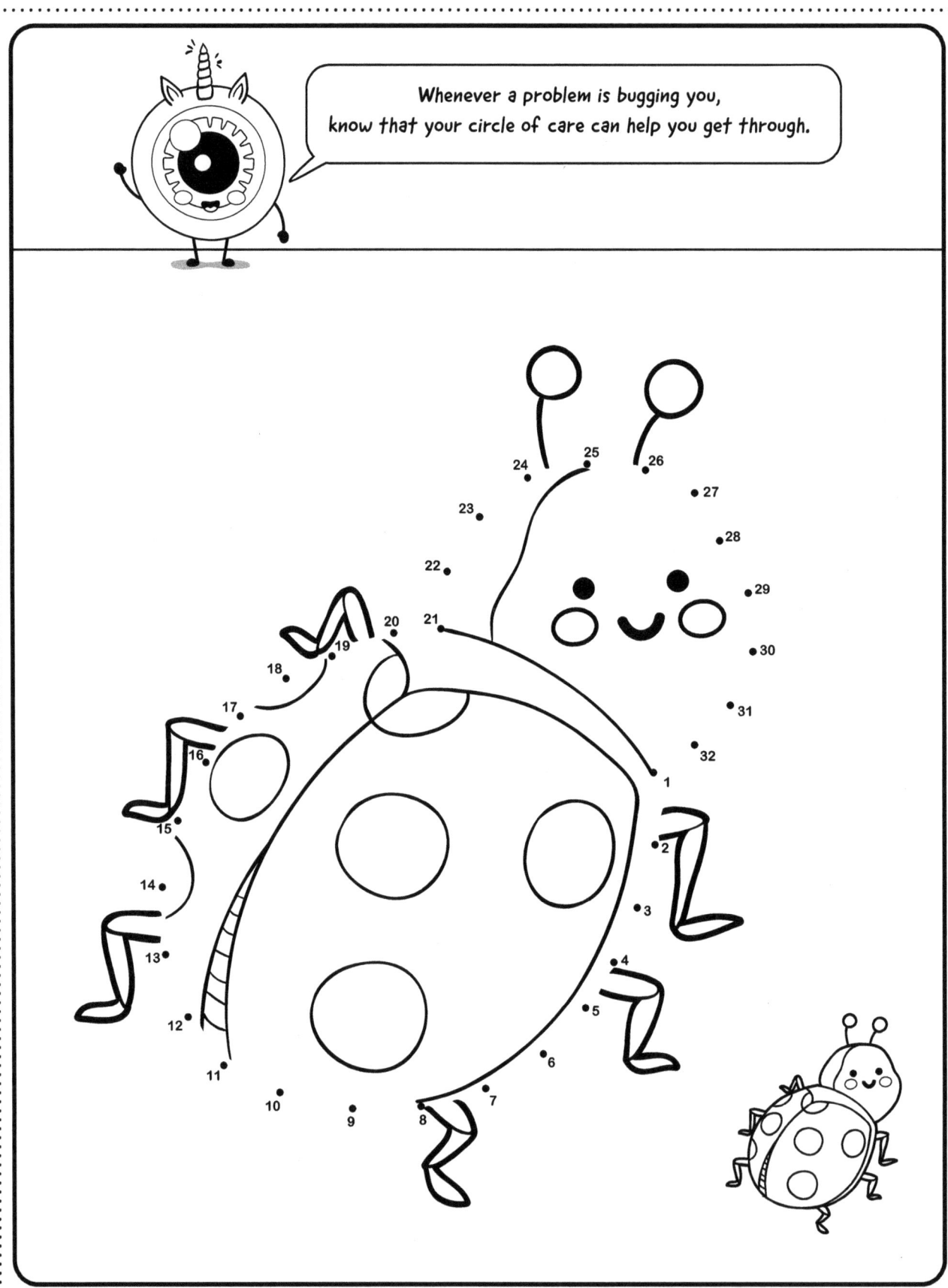

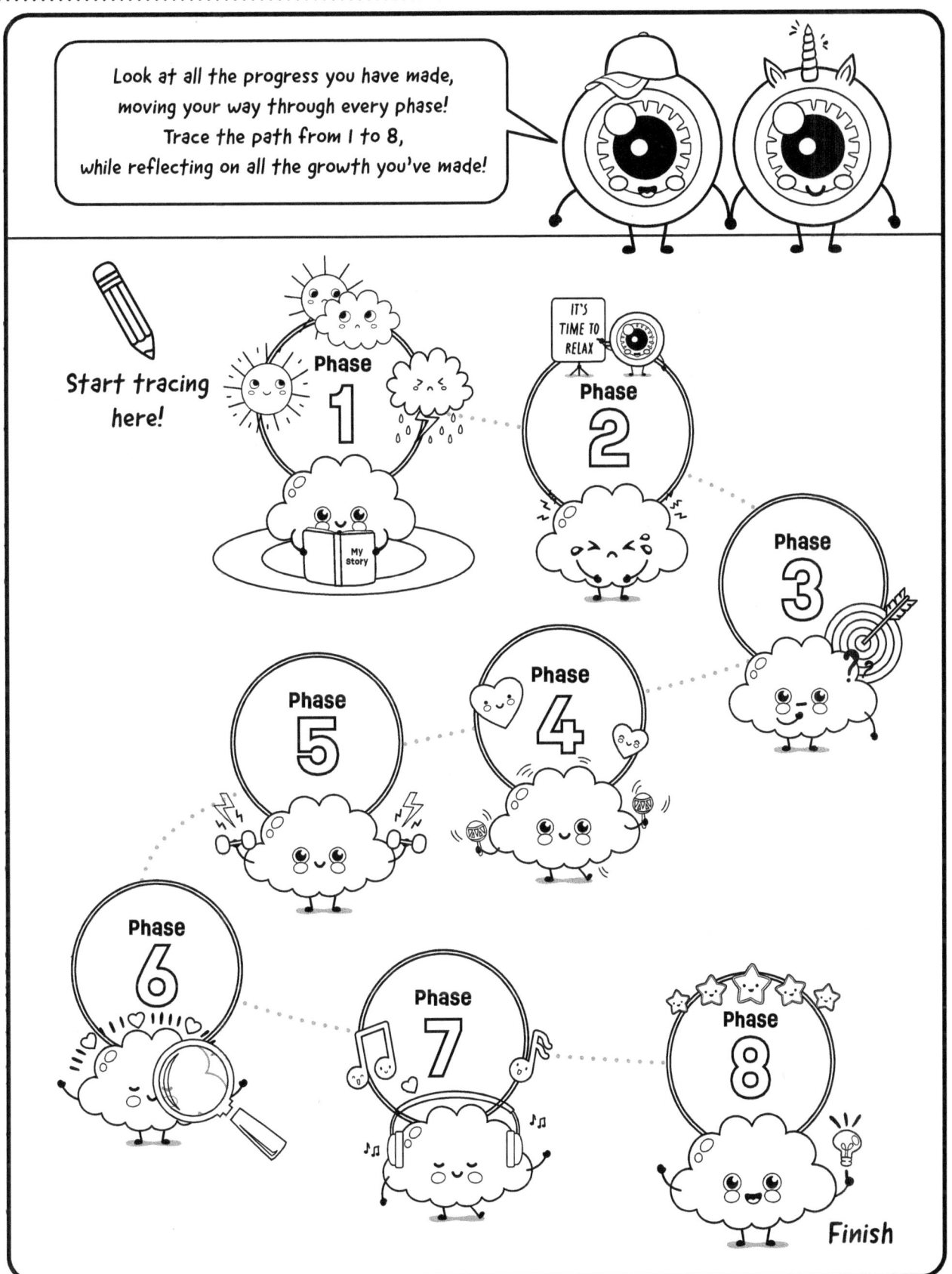

I can do anything I put my mind to

Thanks for letting us help you along the way!

We hope you feel better for all of your days!

About the Author

Christine Mark-Griffin, LCSW, is a certified EMDR therapist and EMDRIA-approved consultant and advanced trainer. As an EMDR consultant and trauma-conscious yoga therapist, Christine is passionate about playfully combining her love of music, movement, fitness, and yoga with clinical practice to help children learn, grow, and heal. She is the owner of Spark All Wellness, a small group practice specializing in EMDR and trauma therapy with women and children. She is also the founder of EMDR for Kids, where the mission is to empower therapists, parents, and children of all ages with resources, tools, and training to overcome trauma and adversity. Christine lives in San Francisco with her husband, two children, and dog. The things that make her happiest include her family and friends, a good cup of coffee, baked goods, yoga, traveling, cycling, music, and dancing.

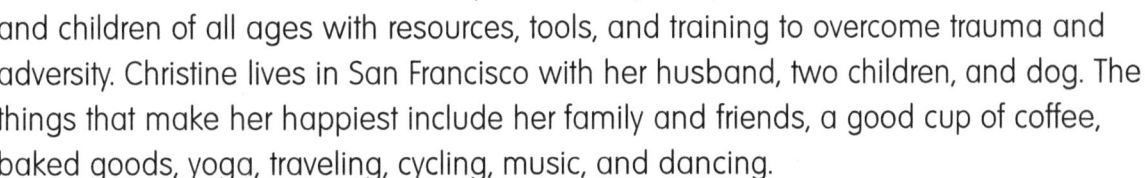

Answers to word search on page 44.

More Great Books for Kids from 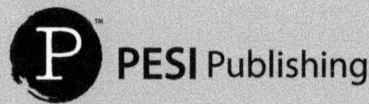 PESI Publishing

Fiona McPhee, Please Listen to Me!
Dr. Katie Hurley, LCSW
A confident, creative girl learns how to harness her assertive nature into strong leadership, celebrating the strengths and contributions of her classmates.

Let's Grow on an Adventure
Lauren Mosback
An anxious young boy gains confidence by exploring the many wonders of nature, his worrisome thoughts growing smaller and smaller with each new discovery.

The Not-So-Friendly Friend
Christina Furnival, MS, LPCC
Children learn an easy and practical lesson about how to firmly and assertively—yet kindly—stand up for themselves in the face of a bully.

When Someone Dies
Andrea Dorn, MSW
Through the lens of mindfulness, children learn how to say goodbye after a loss, make space for any emotions that arise, and work through their grief.

Welcome to Therapy
Andrea Dorn, MSW, LISW-CP
This book walks children through the process of starting therapy in simple, concrete, and developmentally appropriate terms so they can better understand what to expect.

The Small and Tall Ball
Frank J. Sileo, PhD
Oliver feels excluded from his school's "Mother-Son & Father-Daughter Dance" because he has two dads. But then he and his classmates find a way to celebrate diverse families of all kinds.

pesipublishing.com | Follow us on Instagram: @pesipublishing